# The Blackness Continues…

## One Man's Ongoing Mission for Equitable Education

### Peter E. Carter

ISBN-13: 978-1-960727-15-2


Publisher: AAPPEAL, LLC, Cranberry Township, PA
www.eac-aappeal.com

# TABLE OF CONTENTS

# Foreword by Peter "PC" Carter

When my dad first published this book, he was alive to see the impact of his story—and that was a joy in itself. He had always lived his life with quiet determination, breaking barriers and achieving milestones as the first Black person in his schools, his workplaces, and often his entire field. But it was never about recognition for him. He believed that each step he took forward—each challenge he faced, each ceiling he shattered—was a chance to make a path easier for those who would come after him. He also saw the way his journey resonated with so many people, how his words offered encouragement to those facing their own challenges, and how his experiences as a barrier-breaker inspired hope for others walking similar paths.

The response to the first edition of this book was incredible. People from all backgrounds reached out, sharing stories of how his journey inspired them to push through their own challenges, to keep going despite the odds. My dad was deeply moved by this, and I could tell he was proud, not just for himself but for the opportunity to connect with so many readers on such a personal level. My dad passed away a few years after the release of the first edition, unexpectedly and heartbreakingly, while doing what he loved most—spending time with us, his family. It's bittersweet now to revisit these pages, knowing he isn't here to share in the continued life of this book. But I take comfort in knowing that his voice, his wisdom, and his heart live on in these words. And though he's no longer here in physical form to see this second printing, I know that he is here in spirit and thrilled to know his story continues to reach and inspire others.

This second printing holds a special place in my heart. It is a testament to his enduring legacy and a reminder of the impact one life can have on so many. As you read these pages, you'll get to know the man I was so fortunate to call my father—the man who taught me by example to stand tall, to persevere, and to believe in the power of purpose.

My dad's journey is one of courage and resilience, but also of love and generosity. And even though he's no longer with us, his voice still speaks through these pages, reminding us that no matter how tough the road may be, we have the power to leave it brighter for those who follow.

Thank you for reading his story and helping to carry forward his legacy.

Peter "PC" Carter

# Peter E. Carter
Rest in Peace
May 8, 2023

*Photo by Ray Bojarski*

# Chapter 1

## The Second Beginning

So, what does a Catholic sixty-year-old do after his final day of work! He goes to Mass, of course. He first attends the TODAY SHOW with a sign reading Happy Retirement for the nation to see, and then walks to St. Patrick's Cathedral, a mere two New York City blocks away and attends the noonday Mass. The significance of this act was that after the Macy's Thanksgiving Day Parade, my mother always took me to St. Francis of Assisi Church on 32nd Street, where she lit a candle, after reaching deep into her purse for a coin to place in the appropriate slot, and then said a prayer of some sort. To commemorate that act, and to thank her and God for my career, I thought it only fitting to attend Mass at St. Patrick's. My attendance at Mass has been repeated every November 1st for now sixteen years. The other 364 days of the year are Mass-less.

During my Mass attending days, I recall only too well a priest proclaiming from the pulpit of a Catholic Parish in Flatbush, Brooklyn, that the parish was changing, and thus, the base parishioners (the white parishioners) were being asked to contribute more. Other than the four significant religious events for my children, I never set foot in a Catholic Church again, until the first day of my retirement, a period of some 34 years.

Members of the clergy whom I knew and respected admonished me for taking the position which I did, condemning the entire organization for the words and attitude of a racist priest, but after all, I had been sufficiently imbued with those types of "dog whistles" for years. For example, in preparation for one of those religious events for one of my children, my son, yes, the eventual Harvard graduate, was studying for his upcoming Confirmation, and doing an extremely poor job of it. He merely went to the class, and then never did any of the homework. As a result, he was always ill-prepared, causing the nun who was running the classes to ask me in a genuinely concerned voice, "Is he slow? We can alter the lessons for him." Yes, he was the only black child in the preparation class of several Catholic kids who attended public school. I was unaware of his negligence regarding his religious studies, which clearly, he disliked, and I immediately corrected the situation. After all, he was at the top academically in his public-school studies in a white suburban school, and there was no rhyme or reason for there to be a difference here, except of course for lack of interest and motivation. I do not recall a surge of interest, but he immediately became motivated. Like the Roman orator Cicero, I shall pass over in silence the tools utilized to produce motivation.

Let us return to real time from this digression! During the latter part of my career as a Superintendent, I was hired to teach as an adjunct professor at Ramapo College in New Jersey. The "adult" students were candidates for a degree in Education and eager to pursue teaching careers. My academic focus was primarily to share with the students the foundations of American Education. On a weekly basis I preached what I and several scholars believed to be a basic fact. When Alexander Hamilton, James Madison and others of the period decided that the young colonists needed to be educated, they only meant for the white males to be educated, and thus set up the American education system accordingly. Several of my college students took umbrage with that, but too bad. No females, no slaves, no poor people were part of the construct for the formation of American education. With some exceptions, our education system continued in that manner for a century or even two. It is no wonder that certain school districts in America are low performing, based on their socio-economic compositions. It was baked into the cake that certain people were not to be educated.

One of my favorite classes dealt with my assigning the students to watch a college football game and observe closely the racial composition of the players and the racial composition of the tens of thousands of spectators (and the cheerleaders).

Prior to Mr. Carter's Class, my students had never taken note of the stark contrast of the white spectators and cheerleaders with the African American athletes on the field. Could race be a factor in the discussions concerning paying our college athletes?

In one of my more famous lectures as we discussed the teaching learning processes present in our secondary schools was my introduction of what I called the "Prom Factor." Very simply, it dealt with the occasion when, and it does happen, "Omar" asks "Brittany" to be his date for the senior prom. I am sure you get the picture. What a spirited discussion arose during that segment of my instruction! There was one female student in my class whose daughter had posed that reality to her and her husband. Mom was fine with it, Dad not so much. I raised this example as we pondered the reason for the preponderance of segregated schools in our nation. Parents do not want their children interacting with non-like races, although there may be a bit of a lessening of that point of view. The main reason is simply that three letter word beginning with "s" and ending in "x." How ignorant is that! Or maybe not – parents are so protective, often protective of the non-dangerous! In case you are curious about the outcome of the young lady's date for the prom—he was black.

In addition to teaching in the college classroom, one of my duties as an adjunct was to supervise Student Teachers. An undergrad in his/her junior year was assigned to me, and it was my responsibility to observe the student in an actual classroom in an elementary school. This was indeed an exciting aspect of my university teaching experience, which would have far reaching satisfaction for me in my "retirement." I can candidly say that the actual student was at best "C" material as far as teaching was concerned, and did not receive my endorsement to pursue a public-school teaching career. When I chatted with the student after one of her attempts at teaching fourth grade, she shared with me the fact that she was in college to please her mother who was a teacher. As gently as possible, I explained to the student teacher that she needed the desire and interest in being a teacher; it is not hereditary, like cancer. I admonished the student to please seek another field of endeavor for her career. Quite frankly, there are too many students in our schools of education who should not be there. And this young lady was one of them. On the other hand, however, there was the Cooperating Teacher, a

Superstar. She possessed every quality of an outstanding elementary instructor and more. Knowledge, intelligence, kindness, management, preparation are just a few of the qualities I choose to name at this juncture, since we shall be surely returning to MVG later in the book, as she rises from classroom teacher to child study team director to principal to superintendent. We note too for the record, she became a parent of two (after the superintendency) and completed a hard-earned doctoral degree.

I also had the pleasure, after formal retirement, to be hired as an adjunct at the graduate level at Farleigh Dickinson University, where I instructed future administrators in the art of educational leadership. And yes, they, as well as my undergrads of Ramapo, were of the Caucasian persuasion, and I was not. My post-work life continued to be as interesting as the actual 36 years which preceded it. I found that working with the graduate students was not nearly as fulfilling as dealing with the younger, less tainted undergraduate pupils. My aspiring administrators may have been more interested in the salary increase than the responsibility bump, not to mention the increased devotion to the pupils and their teachers. School Administration is an "ALL IN" profession; anything less does not begin to rise to the level of excellence. The highlight of this experience was the opportunity to invite my mentor (VG of Union County days) as a guest lecturer. In addition to the excellent contribution VG made to my class, his third grandson was born while he was teaching. No, I do not take credit for either his stellar delivery or his daughter-in-law's beautiful delivery. Yes, I do take credit for writing the name of the newborn on the chalkboard for all to see.

Upon taking residence in southern Delaware, the current superintendent of the local school district, called the Cape Henlopen School District, resigned, thus creating an opening. Even though I had been admonished by my daughter to curtail full time working activities, like an addict, I answered the advertisement for the position. Either the screening committee could not discern my color from my extensive resume or they needed a "token" as part of the process. Whatever the reason, I was granted an interview. I was interviewed by the Committee which contained a few of the district's administrators, a teacher (union rep) or two, and some prominent citizens. Sitting behind this austere group, but not asking questions or involved at this level of the screening process, were several members of the Board of Education. Quite frankly, I found this a bit strange, but proceeded with the process. I kind of like interviews! After the usual hour, the interview concluded; I knew I had aced it, but this was Sussex County, Delaware.

The white man who was eventually hired as the new superintendent had been recently named as the Superintendent of the Year for the State of Delaware. He was currently the chief school administrator of a small school district even further south in the state than Milton/Lewes/Rehoboth (the component towns which are Cape Henlopen). There was no way in the world that he matched me in experience or scholarship. One of the members of the search/screening committee, a prominent building administrator in the district, later told me that I indeed was the top candidate for the job, but was declared second for obvious reasons. Just as well, I guess; it would have been very tricky explaining to my daughter that I was going back to work full time as a superintendent, having been retired for less than a year.

So, it was made clear to me that I was not in Kansas anymore, but neither anger nor disappointment overwhelmed or even overcame me. I am just not wired that way. There was nothing to be gained from an emotional reaction to yet another occasion of racism. In fact, I spent some time in conversation now and then with the newly hired superintendent, as well as volunteering in the two elementary schools which (at that time) educated the black students in the district. In one school, I became part of a team which supported the reading department; in the other school, I took on the role of a math tutor for one of the building's exceedingly difficult students. Both assignments were rewarding and fulfilling, in that I was able to make a difference in the academic and personal lives of a few students. I also became acquainted with two of the district's talented elementary principals, and the building head custodian and lead secretary in each school.

In my opinion, and in fact, the most important person in a school building is the head custodian, seconded by the lead secretary, followed by the Principal. Ask any good Principal!

I also attempted working at the graduate level at a Delaware institution called Wilmington University, located in the southern part of the First State. The best description of this experience is that it just did not work out. It was not a "fit," either intellectually or racially. This was a bit of a shocker for the man who had defeated and overcome so many obstacles. These particular guys and gals just did not like their black adjunct instructor who knew so much more than they could ever hope to. Welcome to Sussex County, Delaware, I guess!

It may be timely to open a discussion as to "why" I was rejected by the graduate students based entirely on race. Underlying the race reality may have been also my style, which the students may have perceived as a "know it all" classroom presentation. There was no way these southern white students could even begin to accept that any person of my hue knew that much about anything. Furthermore, they apparently had enrolled in other courses which were much less demanding than mine. Since this was not my first academic rodeo in higher education, I approached the job in the manner to which I had been accustomed. My error was the assumption that these adults really wanted to learn something about education and educational administration. What they wanted was three graduate credits in return for their tuition checks. However, my moral integrity drove me to actually instruct these people, or at least to try to impart new knowledge into their brains.

I learned an interesting lesson: not all students are created equal. Not all institutions of higher learning are always about learning. A recently hired adjunct instructor had best learn the prior two dictums early in his employment. It is unfortunate, of course, that such may be the reality of some graduate programs, and I still wonder whether the "push back" against and criticism of yours truly was due less to lack of rigor in the program and more to my race. Could it be that in the minds and hearts of these students, a black person could not be bright enough to instruct them, and thus intellectual resentment was the result? I could not verify my theory since there were no other instructors of color in the education graduate department. Sometimes being a black first or just a black only works against the incumbent.

# Chapter 2

## Delaware – The Location of This Beginning

With my apologies for getting a bit ahead of myself in the first chapter, you need to know the missing pieces between my last day of work and my first day in my brand-new condominium in the First State. I well realized that my New Jersey Pension coupled with United States Social Security would not go as far as I would like in the Garden State, and thus it was sensible to contemplate relocation. I embarked on some research, such as it was, since I am not a research type of person — planning and preparation yes, research, no. The outcome was three states – Texas, Nevada, Delaware. They were the most tax-friendly places in the country at the time. I quickly reached the conclusion that the Lone Star State was not the place for this arrogant man of color for oh so many reasons. I really love gambling, so to move to the gambling mecca of our nation was not a prudent economic decision.

You may recall my best friend, the Irishman with whom I travelled to high school on the New York City subway, and the best man at my wedding (TW); well, he owned a summer residence in a place called Lewes, Delaware, which I visited on several occasions over my years as a Jersey dweller. He, of course, suggested that I relocate to Delaware, and we could grow old together. Since I had lived in Delaware 29 years prior, and survived, I seriously considered such a move. He and his wife hosted me for a week or so in the fall of 2004. I looked at four properties; I made a down payment on one of them, brand new construction named Paynter's Mill built by two young white brothers who had done well on Wall Street. Five months later I moved myself and possessions to Milton, Delaware. It was Memorial Day, 2005. My new home was located 15 driving minutes from the Atlantic Ocean and a delightful town named Rehoboth Beach, 30 driving minutes in the summer months, by the way.

The intervening days between Thanksgiving and Memorial Day were spent preparing for my move from an apartment in Parsippany, New Jersey to a brand-new condominium in Milton, Delaware. I had not owned property since 1973; there was much preparation necessary in these intervening days and months, extracting "stuff" from a storage facility among them. There was also a matter of an automobile, given the reality that my prior employer had provided me with a "company car." For the record, it had formerly been driven by a Ringwood police detective, and little was done to camouflage its appearance. Thus, purchasing it from the district was out of the question. I must admit that the Crowne Victoria was extremely helpful for speedy rides on New Jersey's highways, especially Route 287. However, after some shopping, I procured a Toyota Avalon XLS which I drove with joy and pride for many years. I must confess that I am a bit of a car lover, without too much knowledge about automotive machinery. It was my habit to buy a new car every three years; why buy new tires when a full car would do. I recall during my time as a middle school principal in Delaware (almost 30 years prior to this set of circumstances) buying a car from a dealership owned by the husband of one of my math teachers. Such a deal!

Someway, somehow, I also owned a Ford Escape during my early Delaware 2005 days, which I traded for my first ever Mercedes-Benz, a 2007 ML 350. What is significant with this purchase is not the automobile but the circumstances. It was a rainy day, and I chose to wander through the "local" Mercedes-Benz dealership lot. During my roaming, I was graciously approached by an employee whom I asked, "Are you the Sales Manager?" His (PP) reply was in the affirmative, and we became and remained friends for close to twenty years. Also of interest was the fact that I made a decision on an SUV (first a white one, then a black one) rather quickly, and was asked, "What do you want me to do with this?", referring to the Ford Escape. Our respective responses are irrelevant; what is extremely important is the way I was treated by the management of this dealership, a white middle-aged male. There was never a moment during our encounters when I was regarded as "less than." MY BLACK LIFE MATTERED.

I, or a member of my family, purchased three or four more luxury autos from PP.

Since I have no real hobbies, other than caring for about forty house plants (really 25, there are duplicates and triplicates), I found myself walking on the Rehoboth Beach boardwalk daily. There were many local human beings who also walked daily. A few even said "Good Morning" to this black man from New Jersey. What was noteworthy was that I was the only African American walking on the boardwalk or on the beach in an area which has a 20% black population. More about that later!

Of the few who acknowledged me as a person was the owner of what we in Jersey call a "greasy spoon" eatery, named Gus (now deceased), and the owner of the pizzeria, named Louie. Both men, as I later learned, had migrated from Greece and had started their restaurant enterprises with next to nothing. These were real people. Louie had a bit of an entourage of other white men who congregated on one of the white benches on the boardwalk. I enjoyed chatting with and listening to these gentlemen. Their philosophies certainly differed from mine, but as long as I did not express mine too often, we were fine. As a matter of fact, I think I may have gained some respect for elderly Caucasian men, especially since they did allow me to participate in their reindeer games.

About a block or two away on Rehoboth Avenue is an establishment called Browseabout Books, owned by another white guy, not from Greece, but from New Jersey, and a former teacher. A group of six men of the owner's (SC) ilk gathered there daily, with a myriad of views and jokes. Oh, I forgot, one of the guys was Hispanic. I found that extremely interesting. I spent my time visiting both my boardwalk guys and my bookstore guys regularly. Of note was the fact that the manager of the bookstore is a much younger (and extremely competent) white female (SCK), who provided a place for us to chat and interact on a daily basis. The humor and wit was delightful! What a fantastic way to start a day! These "friends" of the boss were delightful, and I learned so much about my new community from them. The fact that we occupied space for several hours each day is a fitting testimony to the generosity of both owner and manager. This manager whom I had long admired moved to the top of my list of special people.

During one of my walks on the Rehoboth Beach Boardwalk, my cell phone rang. On the other end of the telephone was one of the New Jersey lawyers with whom I had interacted during my years as the Essex County Superintendent. The interaction at the time was somewhat adversarial, but a learning experience for these young black barristers of superior intellect. In fact, I later retained these young men to represent me in a discrimination lawsuit in which we prevailed. One of the State of New Jersey's organizations was not ready for a black first in the leadership role of the organization, and I sued their asses and won. The content of the telephone conversation on the boardwalk involved an invitation to be an Interim Superintendent at one of central New Jersey's urban school districts. I accepted the invitation.

An Interim Superintendent is the person who leads a school district while the Board of Education searches for a permanent person to be hired into that role. The method of selection for an interim varies throughout the profession. One avenue is via recommendation by the Board's Attorney. The Board of this urban school district chose to utilize this method, much to the chagrin of certain political individuals in this community. Several other issues were possibly at play (they usually are), including political toleration for the incumbent, a woman of color.

# Chapter 3

## Six Months in Plainfield, New Jersey

Prior to the completion of my contract negotiations with the Plainfield Board of Education, I made it quite clear that I bring with me two especially important professionals to assist me in the running of the district. WR, who can be called the operations guy, and MD, who takes care of all fiscal and physical plant matters. My leadership style is such that I have my number two person, the Assistant Superintendent, run the place, and I provide the overall leadership in the district and the community. The City of Plainfield, or the Queen City as it is known, is a remarkably interesting sociological construct in that it houses African Americans who are college graduates and fiscally solvent, blacks who are barely (but successfully) making ends meet, and Negroes who look forward to that governmental check monthly. Interspersed in this group of individuals are some white folks who have refused to flee the city for a variety of reasons. The Board of Education was composed of the first two groups, who did give me a unanimous vote at the meeting at which I was hired. I tend not to take a job without a unanimous vote. You may disagree with one another on a myriad of issues, board members, but you must at least agree on my candidacy.

The outgoing Superintendent was, to say the least, a weak leader, but did not realize that, and was extremely surprised that the Board had shown her the door. I will admit that the district was fortunate to have had two outstanding educators prior to the incumbent, possibly making them both hard acts to follow for my poor predecessor. The school district contained one high school, two middle schools, and six or so elementary schools. The "or so" terminology was due to the fact that the State of New Jersey, in its inimitable wisdom, had created a hybrid building to temporarily house and educate children as they awaited the construction of a new school somewhere in the city. My office was located on the second floor of the Administration Building, and my key deputies were on the first floor. I was furnished an automobile of sorts to get around the district.

The women and men who were board members were ambivalent regarding the improvement of instruction in the schools in the district, but my team and I were dead serious that Plainfield could become a model urban school district in New Jersey. In a sense, we were rowing the boat in opposite directions at times.

Dwelling in the district and exercising undue influence was a Representative in the State House supported by the local State Senator. The Mayor of the City, a woman of color, was a pawn of these gentlemen, one of color, one not. The Interim Superintendent was supposedly to be caught in the middle of all this political fervor, but not this Interim Superintendent. Once this reality was made abundantly clear, the forces that could not handle such independence sought to have me removed via a complaint filed with the Department of Education alleging that I had been hired improperly and/or illegally. The crux of the complaint was based upon the fact that yours truly had a prior professional relationship with the law firm representing the school district, the law firm which had sought me out to be the interim. The State did investigate, wrote a report, and I retained my position as Interim Superintendent.

Our first event as a leadership team was the omen of things to come, but WHO KNEW? The 137th High School Commencement was scheduled for six o'clock in the evening on June 21, 2007. At 5:30, the graduating seniors and district officials began lining up at Hub Stine Athletic Field, as did the clouds in the sky. At 5:45, the threat of rain became more visually apparent. As an aside, I should mention that weather forecasters had predicted a chance of rain for later that evening. We started the processional, seated the seniors in their caps and gowns, seated ourselves in our graduation attire, and at 6:10 p.m., as the first set of names were being read by the Vice-Principal, the heavens opened. The graduating students promptly left their seats and sought shelter, as my suit became soaked with the waters from above. Neither the press nor the community was shy with its criticism of the decision-making skills of their new superintendent. Comparisons were made to a neighboring district or two which had moved ceremonies indoors in light of the forecast, not to mention a scathing "letter to the editor" from an aunt of a graduating student who had traveled many miles just to see her nephew receive his diploma, which of course did not happen. The Class of 2007 young gentleman and his 400 classmates did of course eventually (within a day) receive their diplomas. Truth be told, this was the least stressful graduation or promotion exercise of my career.

The boys and girls who attended the public schools under our jurisdiction were primarily from the homes of the hard-working parents and grandparents who toiled at a job or two daily to make ends meet. To assist them in their efforts to raise their families, I made certain that all students were given free breakfast. The school day began with breakfast, and then the Pledge of Allegiance. The students attended "neighborhood" elementary schools which fed into two separate middle schools. The populations of the middle schools reflected the mini communities from which they came, making one middle school much more challenging than the other. I soon found a talented young black lady to run the more troublesome of the two as its Principal. She was terrific! Keep in mind that about 50% of children attending "the other" middle school were from those aforementioned African American college educated, fiscally solvent households. The challenge for both middle school Principals, one, of course, more than the other, was to keep the betweenagers' minds and bodies focused on teaching and learning rather than on each other and their attire (or sometimes lack thereof). I do give the teaching staffs of both middle schools credit for their efforts to instill knowledge about language arts, mathematics, social studies, and science into the heads of the students.

All, actually 75%, of these middle school eighth graders entered a place called Plainfield High School to spend their four secondary school years. The high school was administered by some good men and women, who tried extremely hard to keep the place from exploding, given the nature of the teenage population therein. Even the so-called Honors Classes were wanting in rigor and scholarship and excellence.

On staff daily at PHS were two uniformed police officers, who, I might add, had been given an actual office. Also in the building, and this was a good thing, was a nursery for the newborn to four-year-old children whose mothers (and sometimes fathers) were high school students. Each parent was required to spend one period per day (yes for credit) in the nursery caring for his or her child as well as learning how to care for children in general. I would describe the school day as par for the course of an urban high school, with the usual trials and tribulations inherent in attempting to educate urban youth. The challenge, as stated with the middle schools, is to keep the students focused on the true reason for being in the building – to learn something that they did not know before. Too many of the children are there for social and non-academic reasons, with little or no regard or interest in the subject matter. To ease some of the social and sexual tensions, urban educators impose and enforce dress codes on the students. There are even some school districts where, with parental support, the board has ruled that the students wear uniforms in the elementary and even middle schools. The less seen, the more learned.

As is common in school communities, there was a Student Handbook for the secondary schools in the district, for which staff and students were responsible for its consumption and comprehension. I added a new twist to this phenomenon – a test on the contents of the Handbook with multiple choice responses to each question. Every opportunity to use multiple-choice questions is a plus to assist in better performance on the annual statewide testing. There was a prize for the homeroom with the highest raw score. We not only accomplished better comprehension of the rules and regulations for our schools, but also gave the students more practice in taking tests with multiple choice answers. My experience in other urban communities over many years taught me that in order to improve the performance of our black/brown students, it was imperative that they had practice in taking tests where options were given for each question. The students knew the answer to the sum of 1 & 1, but became confused when "distractors" (such as 11 or 3) were added to the mix. More practice in a variety of school situations yielded higher test scores on the annual state assessments.

And then there was Friday dismissal at Plainfield High School. We brought in the Juvenile Unit of Plainfield Police Department to assist with dismissal. It appeared that threats and other warnings had built up during the five days, perhaps even stares and proposals, and justice was to be physically administered after school on a Friday, almost every Friday. The high school administrative staff tried its best, but there soon came a time, like in a baseball game, that we had to change pitchers. There was only one problem – no bullpen! The solution, and not a great one, was to move the Assistant Superintendent to the high school. We traded a headache for an upset stomach. Nonetheless, the high school students benefitted from this decision in that the climate and the instruction at the high school improved greatly, and we were able to have the police officers spend more time in the office with which they were provided, and not patrolling the corridors "picking up" wayward students.

Well, about those many elementary (Pre-Kindergarten to Fifth Grade) schools! Things were going well there, right? The answer is: on most days. Let me tell you about one of the not so good days. It was a day that I had a bad cold and decided to stay home to rest, a rarity in my career. In the 6,000 workdays (30 x 200), I may have been absent for reason of illness perhaps 5 days. As it turned out, this "sick day" was truly short lived. A fourth-grade student had decided to bring his older brother's gun to school to show it to his classmates. He had the gun, a .45 caliber semiautomatic pistol loaded with one bullet, in his backpack with his other belongings and a few books. It appears that he did show the pistol to a few of his friends, but left it in the backpack. Grandma, yes, the savior of so many urban households in America, possibly noticing that the revolver was missing at home, came to the school "to check on her grandson's grades." Unknown to the Principal, not a superstar by any stretch of the imagination, Grandma, told of the existence of the revolver by another student, went to her grandson's backpack, removed the gun, and took it to the Police Station. Within minutes, the Chief of Police contacted my office via our Director of Security to report that a student had a gun in school, and within seconds my Business Administrator called me at home in my sick bed. Simultaneously, police radio notification must have been transmitted over the air, because when I arrived, tissues in hand for my moist nostrils, I was met by the press, both print and video.

What ensued was a full-throated Press Conference with the Chief of Police, the Director of Public Safety, the Mayor, the politician from the State House of Representatives, and starring the Interim Superintendent. The press and thus the public were told that at no time were any of the children in danger or at risk, due to the fast thinking of the student's grandmother who had noticed the missing revolver. The Press, God bless them, questioned me regarding my expelling the third grader from school. Leaving aside that the law did not permit me to expel a student on the spot, I let the press know that I did not intend to suspend this young child either. "He made a mistake," I said, "and we shall have the guidance counselor and social worker chat with him about making better decisions in his future; the child needs to be and shall continue to be in school." The press was pissed, the police were pissed, the politicians were pissed. The Student and the Superintendent were fine – the way it should be. I dictated a letter to the parents which was sent home that afternoon co-signed by the Principal and yours truly on the school's letterhead stationery.

THE PRESS is an interesting interloper in the life of a Superintendent, with its own agenda – to make the school leader look bad. You recall the June Graduation! Making any government official look bad or even stupid is a good day for The Press. The trick is to look directly into the camera and let the reporter and the viewer know the truth, which is usually not in sync with what the press is trying to unearth. My college days as a sportscaster came in very handy with the Press with whom I had many bouts in print and on air. Once the reporter puts that microphone in front of your face, your mind must move into overdrive or you are doomed. In my earlier urban experience, Irvington, the press came after me on the first day of school because there were long lines of parents waiting to register their young ones for school. A major television station and their star reporter drove from Manhattan to New Jersey to cover this non-story. "Why, Mr. Carter, are these parents waiting for hours to register their children on the first day of school?" I replied quite simply that the parents chose not to register them during the two-week period prior to the day in question because urban parents do not operate that way. They wait until the event is upon them. The days before school opens is for buying school clothes, especially since the government check usually arrives on the first of the month, and we open schools after Labor Day. The Press was intent on painting the school leader as a poor planner because these parents, about 50, had to wait to register their children. Registration is a lengthy process in that it involves documents which prove birth and vaccinations and current address. Sometimes one or more of these documents are not in Momma's pocketbook, and certainly not retrievable from a Safe Deposit Box, whatever that is.

We return now ever so briefly to Plainfield, where the three of us, now called The Dream Team by our supporters, the parents (the middle hard-working group), went to the Board in mid-December to seek an adjustment in our financial compensations for the new calendar year. We sought this not because we were greedy, as was being alleged, but because we were working twelve-hour days and weekends to properly run the district. The members of the Board of Education did not even give us the courtesy of hearing our situation, but instead adjourned the meeting, after holding a closed session from which we were excluded, and publicly walked out. The next morning, at the urging of WR's daughter, we resigned, en masse, effective December 31$^{st}$. We had started on June 1$^{st}$.

Being professional and devoted to kids does not mean or imply that we should be USED. The Plainfield Board of Education, by totally ignoring our request to meet and chat, displayed such gross discourtesy that we were forced to resign. We so wanted to make a difference for the citizens of all ages in the district, but such was not to be the case. Upon our departure the Board appointed one of my employees, the Human Resources Director, as the Interim Superintendent. Clearly that employee had been working *sub rosa* with certain board members to feather her own nest. The comings and goings of certain human beings in some of these school districts leaves so much to be desired. The board also then rehired the former Business Administrator. The Dream Team had been faded into the sunset.

Once again, we proved that there are those forces in our urban school districts who do not want excellence in the education of their children. Some people are too caught up in their own personal and political issues and ambitions and put the children in second or even third place. I put the kids first. After all, "IT'S ABOUT KIDS," which is purposefully the name of my education consulting company. The potential for good education in Plainfield is possible, the potential for great education is reachable, the potential for excellent education is attainable. It was a shame that the people in power did not want us to help Plainfield realize its potential. It was more than a shame; it was sad. We really wanted to make a major difference for the thousands of students who called themselves Cardinals.

# Chapter 4

## R & R in Rehoboth Beach, Delaware

To set the stage chronologically, it is January of 2008, and I have nothing to do. The first third of the year was spent primarily visiting doctors in Delaware and some Broadway theaters in Manhattan, attending the wedding of the daughter of one of my former secretaries, and even going on a trip or two to Atlantic City. One of the triumphs of free time is the ability to reflect on a few of one's activities of the past. A special and unique place of reflection and inspiration is on the treadmill in the cardiologist office, followed some days later by a trip to the catherization lab for perhaps yet another stent. Lying on a medical table as a cardiology team inserts an instrument into one's groin, the termination point of which is the heart, could give one "pause." The outcome of the procedure was positive in that the doctors affirmed the previously diagnosed total blockage in one artery and about a 20% blockage in the other. I could, and did, live with that for ten plus more years. Good drugs were prescribed, and my daily walks on the boardwalk proved to be health inducing.

As I enjoyed the Atlantic Ocean and the people who deemed to acknowledge me during my daily constitutional, I gave myself the luxurious opportunity to think about the years I had spent in education, and what were (and are) the challenges therein. Perhaps the primary reality is that professional public education is political. Schools and school districts are complex political and legal constructs. They are run by men and women who are elected on a statewide basis, and women and men elected (or in some places appointed) at the local level. There are many people involved before we even get to a desk or textbook, and these people know truly little about either desks or textbooks. In fact, very few of these elected officials have any idea how education really works. How do we professionals impart information and knowledge into the minds of children? Fortunately, the people who are actually doing the work on a daily basis have been trained and educated to do just that — trained in so many cases by their professional elders who are sincerely thanked herein. I will admit that some of us do the work better than others, and in fact some are very poor at the job. The children and parents are extremely thankful that most of us are really good at what we do.

How does one gain such prowess, you ask? In the same manner as a Tom Brady or a LeBron James or a Sandy Koufax or a Serena Williams. You practice, you practice, you practice some more. Along the way, there are excellent coaches and mentors. Thus, you listen, you listen, you listen some more, all the time remembering that it is the child who is the most important member of the equation. Is what you are doing, or just did, or about to do, GOOD FOR KIDS?

And yes, to return to the sports comparison, you win. It is an ongoing contest between administrator and whomever else is trying to make you fail: Board members, local and state politicians, the press, the parents, and even your colleagues and employees. The trick, whether you be Belichick or Arians, is to overcome whatever the opposition throws at you, and get the ring on that Sunday in February. It is the preparation and the practice which produce the reward of that Lombardi

Trophy. Every day of that twelve-hour workday leads to that.

Thoughts, frustrations, triumphs traveled through my brain during 2008 as I wondered whether I had left the profession too soon. There was still so much left to do, despite what my daughter had said about "enough." She was right of course; the job should not be done with only one of the heart's arteries, and if one is black, you need an extra artery. Quite fortunately, I have been blessed with above average intelligence, and to do this education thing with any semblance of success, you must be smart, very smart. Unfortunately, though, the very bright opt not to become involved in education. Their reasons are sound – money, control, patience. Not enough of the first, too much of the second, and a dearth of the third. Wall Street, NASA, Johns Hopkins, and Law call out to the academically talented, leaving Education to the few and far between. I am the only educator from my High School graduating class of 157, and only three of us from the college graduating class of 1500 entered the profession, and only one went into the world of K-12. I recall too well being chastised by classmates for choosing education as my profession. Classmates nothing! My mother, remember her, was not that thrilled either. But let us move on. I was thrilled and proud, and good.

In addition to my attempt to be an adjunct instructor at Wilmington University in Sussex County, Delaware, I tried my hand at a leadership role in my local Condo Association. Interestingly enough, I was well received by my [all] white neighbors, so much more so than by the [all] white students at the college. I was one of the first owners in this beautifully landscaped community and became quickly respected as a retired school official from New Jersey. I served on the board of one of the secondary communities as well as what we can be called the master community. It was fun and a pleasure to be able to contribute to my new Milton, Delaware surroundings. I was at the table with the builder and developer when we successfully negotiated good things for our owners, and I worked closely with the management company to procure the best services for the fees being charged. I even sat across the table from the most prominent landscaper in the area to prevent his company from charging us for erroneous claims (a damaged plow, for example). I cannot surmise what produced success in a real estate environment and failure in Delaware higher education, other than my white neighbors were nowhere nearly as white as my white graduate students.

To answer the question indirectly just posed, I believe that my neighbors supported this black man because many of them had retired from jobs which required intelligence and graduate school credentials. It is true that the more advanced the academic degree, the less the chance of bigotry and racist orientation. It is also interesting to note that white men and women with college plus credentials probably have met people of color who held similar degrees, and thus respect for an African American is more present than with the average non-higher degreed white person. Aretha Franklin said it and sang it, R-E-S-P-E-C-T.

Concurrently, of course, I have and had respect for my neighbors, and consequently let them know that THEY MATTER as we made decisions on behalf of the community. This mode of behavior was to serve me well as you, the reader, shall learn a bit later in the book. The Year 2008 ended with my visiting my original cardiologist in New Jersey for a consult and undergoing a cardiac catherization procedure at Delaware's Beebe Hospital. Four stents if you are keeping score.

So, I was instructed to take it easy and enjoy the waves and the sunshine, but there is little sunshine in the winter, and the place, as I shall note in the next chapter, is rather desolate, or at least it was up until about 2010. So take it easy I did: Read a book here, visited a museum there, played some slots at the casinos at other times, and realized that climbing stairs to my second-floor condominium might not be a highpoint in my retirement.

# Chapter 5

## Finding Something to Do

Those daily walks of two miles each on Rehoboth's Boardwalk proved to be not only quite cardiologically beneficial but also economically advantageous. During the winter months in Lower Slower Delaware (that's what the natives call the area), there is absolutely nothing to do, or shall we say very little to do. The skies are grey, nightfall comes early, the birds are gone. On the upside, there is much less traffic, as compared with the summer months. I am speaking primarily about January and February. It is so dark and desolate at times, thoughts of returning to New Jersey often ran through my mind. Then I balanced that thinking with the cost of living in the Garden State. Needless to say, I remained in the First State. My involvement with the Homeowners Association took up a considerable amount of time and continued to be fun and interesting. I learned quite a bit about how southern Delaware worked and how informal many of the "deals" were, given our inability to find actual documents with respect to construction specifications and relationships among building vendors. I learned so much and met many movers and shakers in the overall process of planning and building homes. What was of considerable interest to me was the lack of new building projects which could be affordable to lower income people of color. In fact, the builders were encouraging those initial black homeowners to sell their properties without the hope or guarantee of replacing what they had sold with a new home. In other words, people who had been here since the days of the Underground Railroad were being taken advantage of. Quietly, I persuaded a fair number of my brothers and sisters not to sell, but to repair and keep the homesteads which had been with their families for years. After all, there were no mortgages on these existing properties.

The interracial relationships among the residents in some of the rural towns are interesting. We have the pure hard-core rednecks whose white supremacism is present, but since poverty prevails, they truly have little power. However, and this is amazing, also because of poverty, there are towns where the offspring of slaves and slaveholders are remarkably close, close as to even intermarry, have barbeques, and cohabit without a problem. Since the schools were integrated in the 1960s or so, the black and white children all go to the same schools. The grandparents enjoy peaceful coexistence with one another and enjoy fried chicken, corn bread, and chitlins, as do the parents. To repeat, they enjoy one another and, in many cases, share similar surnames.

I spent the spring traveling around the western portion of the state which is called Sussex County. This is corn and watermelon country, and let us not lose sight of the poultry. Yes, there is a large Perdue plant down here and Mountaire Farms and naturally thousands of chickens. Of greater sociological interest is the fact that the human beings who work daily to bring chicken from the coup to the supermarket are from Spanish speaking Central America. The test scores of the school district which encompasses these plants reflects the social condition of the children of our plant workers. The same is true, even more so, of the offspring of the watermelon harvesters. By the way, readers, the chicken and the watermelon and the corn are absolutely delicious.

My Central American brothers and sisters are also employed by the landscaping industry, of which there are three major companies and about seven minor ones. The white men quickly realized that, with the rapid housing development, there would be a need for lawns to be manicured and irrigated. Of course, the labor for these companies is provided by minorities who perform their duties in an excellent manner. So, one is reminded of the slaves who harvested cotton for "Massa." The obvious difference is that these workers are brown, not black, and they are paid, not that much, but they do collect wages.

The population of my friends from Guatemala and neighboring countries is not that considerable, and thus they have no economic or political clout, at least not yet. I am hoping that very soon there will be a BROWN FIRST.

As the months wore on, it was soon May and June once again, time to stop my informal and non-scholarly sociological study. It was time to walk on the boardwalk, smiling and nodding and strengthening my cardio. Guess what happened again? Yes, that cell phone of mine rang. On the other end, another one of my New Jersey attorneys was calling, somewhat desperate for me to consider yet another interim superintendency and save an ailing school district.

# Chapter 6

## Last Stop on the Interim Train: HOBOKEN

The use of the word train is so meaningful in that Hoboken is the hub for transportation from New Jersey to New York, Manhattan to be specific. The New Jersey Transit Station in Hoboken is the hub from which passengers from over fifty towns in the Garden State transfer to the once famous "Hudson Tubes" for transport into the Big Apple. For those who wish to avoid the hassle of changing from one train to another and who can afford the fiscal investment, there is residence in the City of Hoboken itself. Those fortunate enough for this commuting bonus can walk, take a bus, or even bicycle to the Hoboken Terminal and board the train which runs under the Hudson River. When I arrived in Hoboken, it was no longer called the "Hudson Tubes." The train to NYC was (and is) called PATH (Port Authority Trans Hudson.) A resident can even take a ferry to the City. This is one busy place, and only four-square miles of land mass. The majority of the citizens are under forty years of age, work on Wall Street, and live in luxury type apartment condominiums. Most of these young people are not parents [yet] and have no idea that in the western part of the city, 2,000 children are being educated. The city also has a large number of taverns and many outstanding restaurants and is protected by a 123 member police force. One of the establishments is a Bakery, known nationally for its outstanding pastries, where the citizens of means line up every weekend to purchase its sweets and goodies. The taverns and restaurants are also quite busy on the weekend evenings and nights.

The City of Hoboken sports a beautiful park on the riverfront. Of utmost importance, unknown to many, the city is topographically located below the Hudson River, making for interesting outcomes after heavy rainfalls. It borders Jersey City with a view of the Statue of Liberty, of which only about half of the school population (both adults and children) is aware. This is one beautiful, but crowded place. Among the residents in the aforementioned condos was a Hall of Fame professional football player, an internationally famous radio personality and spouse, and several other millionaires, also unaware of an educational enterprise coexisting with their bank accounts and investments.

With all this beauty and wealth on the acreage west of Washington Avenue, one would think that the school district would be stellar. On the contrary, it was a mess! August/September 2009, yours truly enters to restore dignity and class to the home of Frank Sinatra, or at least to the school system.

The monthly meetings of the Board of Education had been contentious and loud and long. So it was for the first meeting I attended! There was a member of the Hoboken Fire Department who had worked part time and temporarily in some capacity for the school district, and had not received the agreed remuneration. This "gentleman" was angry and agitated and connected. After his Academy Award performance, I spoke with him, and assured him that he would be paid for his services to the school district, but his part time services, whatever they were, were no longer needed. There were three or four people of interest in attendance at the meeting, who expressed their individual points of view on matters which had occurred or were occurring in the district. Board members (all nine of them) were vocal too. The meeting, which began at 8:00 pm, ended a little after midnight; such never happened again. I informed the Board that night that my brain stopped operating at 10:00 pm and so would subsequent board meetings.

The purpose of the monthly meeting of a Board of Education is for the trustees of the public's monies to approve matters of personnel and expenditures which involve such dollars. The job of the Superintendent is to properly prepare the board members in advance with the facts which impact upon their decision making. The challenge in Hoboken was the reality that several of the board members had agendas which had little to do with the education of Hoboken's public-school children. The board members had also been spoiled by my predecessor, who was a resident of the city and frequently succumbed to their wills and needs. We shall leave that topic alone and focus on the preparation of which I spoke. Hours upon hours and written lines upon lines occurred for as much as two weeks prior to each and every board meeting. I recall a particular matter which caused me to meet with four board members on a Sunday afternoon to avoid a confrontation at a subsequent meeting. By the way, more than a decade later, I may still hold the record for one of the shortest Hoboken Board meetings at 53 minutes.

To use the word "corrupt" would be an understatement, but I shall let you, the reader, judge for yourself as I relate a few incidents which occurred, or, in some cases (thank goodness), did not occur. There was a Department Supervisor who had been promised a promotion of some sort by the prior administration (actually administrator). It was very unclear as to the qualifications of this individual for this so-called promotion into a position which did not even exist. I did believe that she had been considered for this raise in status and salary, and was undoubtedly persistent in her quest. However, such did not occur. The employee, after some weeping and gnashing of teeth, subsequently resigned and moved to California.

Public entities are subject to corrupt behaviors, given the monies involved and the notion that no one will notice a bad habit here or there. Temptation is rampant, and many public officials believe they will never be detected or caught. What is so shameful with respect to schools and school districts is that with each act of misbehavior, the criminal involved is stealing from the children. Whether the offense is goods or services, it is still disgusting for adults to take anything which has been designated for the students. However, such thievery is all too rampant, even small infractions, like soap, towels, t-shirts, hot dogs. Then there is the big stuff, more so at the college level, but present in K-12 nonetheless: footwear, equipment, game tickets, student favors. These are general examples and not necessarily germane to Hoboken, but worth mentioning in a section about corruption in an educational enterprise where that menace can seep in. Athletics is but one of the areas where corruption can be observed, but it can run rampant through all parts of a school district if not stopped where it exists and then controlled.

The Hoboken Board owned several school buses. The purpose of a school bus is for the transportation of pupils from home (or a day care center) to a certified educational facility within or outside of the geographical boundaries of the school district, and the return of said pupils to home or a day care center. For the record, karate school and ballet practice do not count as legitimate destination points for a taxpayer supported vehicle. In Hoboken, prior to my arrival (a period of time affectionately known in several school districts as BC-Before Carter), the Boys Scouts had been taken to their summer camp activities by School District vehicles. Imagine that!

Fortunately, word of this practice came to my attention days before the annual trip, and unfortunately for the Boys Scouts' people, I said "no more" of that. A very angry scout leader, a mom, stormed into the administrative offices to inquire as to who stopped the wheels from turning. Upon learning it was the Superintendent, and then seeing the Superintendent, she met me with the question, "Who the hell do you think you are? We have been doing this for years." My response was "I am the Interim Superintendent of Schools." There were other words exchanged, more on the part of the mom than yours truly, few of which can be written here. The confrontation ended with her storming out of the offices on her way to the mayor's office, with a stop, I believe, at our Transportation Office. That was the end of that corrupt practice. No, I have no idea how the Boys Scouts eventually got to camp, and guess what, Clark Gable as Rhett Butler in *Gone With The Wind* said it best.

It appeared that Transportation was the most vulnerable department for misdeeds. There had been another "thing": chosen female residents of the city were driven in the school buses to the local Super Market (actual name purposefully withheld) to procure their groceries for the week. I heard of this "service" by chance, and thus actually followed a bus on its rounds picking up passengers and taking them to the supermarket. Yes, I waited for them to return to the School Bus with their groceries, and then be driven back to their respective homes. This was time extremely well spent, resulting in the termination of a few members of the Transportation Department. Other specific or internal details shall be withheld for all the proper reasons. I will mention that the supermarket in question was franchised owned by a prominent and wealthy member of the Hoboken community.

That particular member of the community had been generous with his money for several projects for the students. His largess was indeed appreciated, as well as his ability to keep segments of the community calm during contentious issues at board meetings. He also engaged me several times in conversation with respect to jobs or promotions for his friends or family members. The conversations were merely that, no personnel outcomes. Many years after I left the school district, the gentleman was arrested for wrongdoing with regard to a variety of his activities.

Then there was a member of the Board of Education who caused an order to be placed with a local sporting goods store for some equipment for one of the high school teams. Unknown to me at the time was that there had been a relationship for years with this store between the board member, an athletic administrator, and the store's owner. Goods seemed to flow into the Athletic Office with and without invoice, and somehow school district checks were written and taken to said store. On one occasion, where there was an invoice of sorts, the number of items actually received by the athletic administrator differed from the number of items listed on the invoice. I personally intercepted the delivery and made the count. Needless to say, there was no more of that.

We shall have a cessation in prose about the wrongdoings of district staff, citizens, and elected officials so that we can begin to focus on, of all things, teaching, learning and instruction. Remember that part of a school and school district? To assist me, I persuaded the Board to hire my number one assistant (WR), whom we have met before. In addition, I brought on as Business Administrator (RD), one of the (if not THE) best in the State of New Jersey. As reinforcement in the fiscal area, the Board also allowed me to hire the special sauce of the Carter triumvirate, MD. The person I met serving in the role of Business Administrator had to be terminated by means of resignation for reasons of gross incompetence and stupidity.

# Chapter 7

# Inside the Hoboken Educational Experience

Much to the surprise of so many residents of the city, there are five buildings in which boys and girls gather five days a week for 180 days from September to June each year. Let us start with the High School, given that was [is] the most interesting of the buildings. When we arrived in the district, the high school educated students in grades nine through twelve and moreover fielded athletes at the same grade levels. I mention athletics at the outset because it was difficult to discern which was more important for the students and parents – academics or athletics. The Football Coach was just as important as the Principal, perhaps even more so. Every Saturday, hundreds gathered to watch the 11 plus 11 football players and the cheerleaders display their skills and bodies. They even came to see and hear the school marching band, about which more shall be written later. During my superintendency, a State Championship was obtained. Hurrah for Hoboken! Not that many entries were gained into Harvard or Yale or Princeton or even Stevens (in town), but still, hurrah for Hoboken.

Students sort of sauntered to class during the school day and enjoyed their lunch. Lunch was hugely enjoyable in that the children were permitted to leave campus daily and eat at one or more of the numerous restaurants (yes, including McDonald's) in the city. Surprisingly, especially to me, all the students returned to the building after lunch every day. I am not a proponent of having teenagers roam all over a town during the noonday hour. Such seems to me to be asking for trouble. However, the students handled that responsibility quite well, in fact even better than merely getting to class within the building in a timely manner. The curriculum was nothing special and quite basic for a suburban/urban high school. I added suburban in my description because the city was home to so many wealthy individuals. There was one area, however, where Hoboken excelled – Drama. The children were extremely talented in the arts and performed at a level almost equal to the professionals who worked across the Hudson River on Broadway. To maintain the theatrical status of the district, once again a bit of corruption seeped into to the mix. The Drama Teacher, and thus the Theatrical Director, was an extremely talented person but did not hold the New Jersey State certificate required to teach drama, nor the credentials to be considered a supervisor or director. The performances were excellent, the legality was not. After months of tussle and bustle, there came a point in time when I had to stop the bleeding and the employment of the director. This was a lose/lose situation for all concerned, including the students who, by the way, had been hosted by this employee at parties at the teacher's home.

Another employee of note was the High School Principal, who held a doctoral degree from Columbia University. The prestigious degree notwithstanding, this staff member lacked the skills to properly administer a secondary school. She was directly supervised by my Assistant Superintendent, whose memos and emails spoke to her weaknesses. She even had difficulty properly dismissing the school from a pep rally at the end of a school day with the entire staff present to assist in said dismissal. There came a point in time when I had to pull the trigger, but prior thereto, this employee submitted a written resignation and was off to assume an administrative position in another school district. Some days before her "last day," I confiscated the district's computer which had been assigned to her in order to protect the district's hardware and software assets. This act was met with great displeasure, including the dispatching of her male friend to my office to procure a non-existent thumb drive. Short of arrest, he changed his aggressive demeanor and departed from the administrative building.

The ex-principal subsequently sued me for gender discrimination, even though she had actually resigned from the position. For the record, we hired an incredibly talented female as the permanent successor high school principal.

There are one or two stories about the pupils and their antics that are worthy of prose. One concerns graduation and cultural differences. In order to make Commencement Exercises much more audience/parental friendly, we altered the seating of the graduates so that they faced the people who had attended to celebrate their achievement. Whether it was that alteration, or just a bad day, one of the straight students whose religion forbad gay/lesbian interactions attacked one of the gay students during the processional. He was duly arrested and taken to jail, still attired in his cap and gown. The irony here is that the high school was populated by a substantial number of LGBTQ beautiful boys and girls, all of whom peacefully coexisted on a daily basis.

The other story, also unfortunately involving law enforcement, is a little more bizarre. A subject area teacher had given the students an assignment which involved costuming in a variety of styles and genres. The students were to bring their creations with them into the building and change once they entered the building. One student, who just happened to be the child of an employee of the district, decided to don his costume at home and come to school so attired. The outfit involved camouflage clothing and a toy gun. To add insult to injury, he further decided to enter the building from a side door. Stationed close to his entry of choice were two sheriff's deputies with real guns and real badges. Upon observation of what appeared to be an intruder or potential mass shooter, the officers sprang into action, guns drawn. Fortunately, (and with God's intervention), no one was injured or died. Indeed, the student was suspended from school for ten days. Expulsion was considered by the board, given the grave situation in which the student had placed himself and classmates. We were incredibly lucky that the deputies had been well trained and exercised intelligence and restraint. It was also fortunate that yours truly and my assistant had established positive rapport with the various branches of law enforcement which patrolled Hoboken.

We had the 123 members of the Hoboken Police Department, several members of the PATH Police, the Hudson County Sheriff's Officers, and, of course, the New Jersey State Police all protecting and serving the City of Hoboken. I even had three local cops assigned to the schools, one of whom was the daughter of the Chief of Police. Yes, Dorothy, we are in Hoboken!

We cannot leave the high school without mentioning once again the Marching Band. Upon arrival at the district, I noticed that the band wore white T-shirts and a type of uniformed trousers. There was no way that students from a district I headed would be on display attired in that manner. One of my first major expenditures was the purchase of real band uniforms, complete with headgear for the drum major, and sharp looking red uniforms for the *Rockin' Redwings*. The kids looked great in the numerous Hoboken parades and programs in which they performed.

Last, but by no means least, was the generosity displayed by the then quarterback of the New York Football Giants through his foundation. The Foundation awarded $25,000 for the purchase of technology related items from the Samsung Corporation, personally presented to the Interim High School Principal and three representative students at the Time Warner Building in

Columbus Circle in Manhattan. Even transportation to the event was provided by a Time Warner Minibus. There are not enough "thank you's" for this now retired Hall of Fame professional athlete, who, by the way, was a Hoboken resident at the time. In fact, I occasionally ran into him and his party at one or more of the city's outstanding restaurants.

For the record, as may have been stated, there were a few other famous people residing in the city, including a famous "shock jock," whose fiscal attention I was unable to obtain, but then again, I probably ran out of time to properly woo them. There was an initial challenge of an absentee employee who was allegedly in charge of curriculum and instruction. This individual, with a doctorate no less, was overseas when we arrived in the district but was still drawing a salary. It appeared that he was submitting some sort of "work" electronically for which he was compensated. After several months of "backwards and forwards," I was able to relieve him of his instructional duties and create a vacancy. The young man whom we hired into the position was excellent, bringing a well needed stimulus into the curriculum as well as to the development of the teaching staff.

The individual schools themselves were interesting. There were five buildings. One building, the farthest from the River, but clearly built lower into the ground, would flood in its basement after every substantial rainfall. The cafeteria was located in the basement, meaning that we could not serve a hot lunch on those days, not to mention the mold and mildew ever present in that part of the building. Fortunately, the elementary kids enjoyed the peanut butter and jelly we had to feed them on the flooded days. This would be an excellent time to discuss the ethnic composition of the schools, since the building about which we are speaking educated the black and brown population. It just so happened that the public housing where the brothers and sisters resided was also in this part of the city. The academic achievement between the students in this building and the others was a chasm, not a gap, not to mention the caliber of the principal. We were fairly successful in making alterations to both. Then there was a magnificent building with a grand staircase which housed a unique group of students, some with special needs, some without, which also needed talented leadership which we provided. We never had the time, unfortunately, to truly stabilize this educational institution which also attempted to educate the children at the elementary grades. On the plus side, Hoboken, being as small as it was in square miles, gave us the flexibility of moving certain children from one school to another without any pushback from the parents. Let me refine that just a bit. We had that flexibility among certain schools, not all.

We now come to a building located literally in the center of a block, with single family homes on either side and across the street, which also educated elementary graded children. This was a small school in square footage, and thus had a relatively small number of students, all of whom lived within walking distance, of course. I trust you get the picture. Not too many black or Hispanic kids attended school in that building, and the instructional outcomes were indicative of the sociology.

For some reason, which I never understood, there was also a type of middle school which educated the children in grades 8, 7, and 6, perhaps even 5. This school was part of the building in which the Superintendent's and Business Offices were located. The Principal of this school was well positioned and ensconced in the operations of the City of Hoboken, and was waiting his turn to be named the successor superintendent. However, the board hired me. Little more need be said or written with regard to that relationship. White men really hate to be supervised by a black man, and absolutely detest to be denied a position which is then given to an African American. Such reality is further enraged if one believes that he was "next." An example of this administrator's "in" with the townsfolk was the fact that the Police Chief assigned his daughter (yes, she was a cop) to that school as the resource officer. What safer place for the boss' daughter than a public school!

Despite my setting the scene of this school in a somewhat questionable light, it functioned very well, although it was overcrowded and utilized some portable classrooms in order to educate the total racially and socially diverse population. Student performance was acceptable, and despite the disappointment and anger and jealousy of the principal, he was an adequate school leader.

As we surveyed the needs of the district, a decision was made with the approval of the Board of Education to move the eighth graders to the high school building to alleviate the density of the population of the so-called middle school. So, on the first anniversary of the Carter Administration's arrival in Hoboken, there was an 8-12 high school for which we provided an excellent transition for both the students and their parents, with some grumblings from the white fathers fearing for the defrocking of their daughters somewhere during the school day, I suppose. Such anxiety was fueled by the male upper-class population, who let the community know that they were looking forward to welcoming these young girls and boys.

It took some doing, but we put a kibosh on the story. There were several meetings with parents, the seventh graders, and, most importantly, my "hands off" meeting with the then eleventh and tenth grade boys. They got the message, loud and clear.

We arranged for a wing of the high school to be devoted to middle school studies, with staff carefully assigned to work with these most delicate of students. We also carefully sowed the seeds for the building to eventually become a 7-12 institution, thus giving even more space at the prior housing for seventh and eighth graders, and the eventual exit of the district offices from that building. By the way, did I mention that Hoboken High School contains an Olympic size swimming pool? One of my goals for the district was that every graduate would be able to swim by the conclusion of his/her high school experience. Another goal was the distribution of laptop computers to all students in the upper grades. The important word is "goal."

# Chapter 8

## Getting Out of Hoboken – Not Easy Either

My contract with the Board of Education was for a one year per diem stint with supplemental compensation for evening meetings. I must say that this was quite pleasant and welcoming for my bank account, even though I had to provide lodging and meals for myself. On that front, I found a well-maintained motel chain managed by an efficient innkeeper, who even gave me the same room for the time I was a part-time resident of the County of Hudson. I returned to Delaware every other week to water my house plants and do my laundry. I found a wonderful dry cleaner who took care of my dress shirts and suits. Both the motel and the cleaners were run by men who had immigrated to our country, as had I. Those weekends I did not drive home to Delaware, I spent in New York City. How wonderful was that! In Manhattan (or Brooklyn or The Bronx) every other weekend for a year or so. On those weekends, I stayed in the neighboring town of Jersey City adjacent to the Holland Tunnel, taking the PATH into the City.

The Board and the people of Hoboken were so pleased with the change in direction of the school district that I was renewed as the interim for an additional six months. This also gave the Board more time to search for a permanent superintendent. Under the rule of a very unpopular and unpleasant governor, the State Government had placed a "cap" [upper limit] on superintendents' salaries. Even a formula had been devised for these salary restrictions, which we shall not even try to explain on the pages of this sequel. Let it be said, though, that the "cap" made it exceedingly difficult to lure candidates to apply for the top jobs in school districts. The Governor, a man of some girth, did not appreciate the reality that many of us superintendents had been making more in salary than he was. We worked harder than he did and deserved to make more money than His Honor.

Speaking of the Governor, let me share with you the fact that I had worked in the State of New Jersey for enough years to have known five governors prior to the one in question here. This guy just did not like the public schools and those of us who administered them. There came a point in time when "His Lordship" visited a charter school in Hoboken for some type of press event. His advance people requested two stools for the presentation, which the host venue did not own. I was asked to loan the school some stools, and, fortunately, I did have furniture of that nature which could sustain the weight of the State's Chief Executive Officer.

I attended the meeting and, as an audience member, asked a question. The question was framed in Rodney King vocabulary, seeking to find out why we all couldn't get along – public schools, private schools, charter schools. The anger and venom which came forth in the form of an answer from the Governor was amazing. Even the members of his own party in the room were embarrassed at the manner in which he spoke to the Superintendent. No, I did not rush the stage and take my stools away, but I did think about it. The other stool, by the way, was occupied by an educational opportunist of some national renown. So much for my sixth Governor, who, in addition to his "cap" thing, had reduced the State Aid to public schools by millions of dollars.

Let us return to my exiting Hoboken, shall we. Eventually the Board found a candidate willing to work in the city. Actually, they found two, but the first one was just a little too dandy for the job, although several board members, one in particular, grew quite fond of him. I shall skip the details of his overall demeanor, other than to share the fact that he had fresh flowers daily on his desk in his current job and trousers with a very well-defined crease. Fortunately for all concerned, he declined the job offer for reasons I never really understood. The other candidate, working in a district where the "cap" was not a factor (I told you it was complicated.) was offered a contract which he accepted but had to be approved by the State's Executive County Superintendent. Even before we reached that final step, legal papers changed hands and offices between the law firm representing the Hoboken Board of Education and the Deputy Attorney General of the State of New Jersey. These two entities had gotten into the weeds on this issue, and rightly so. However, it was time for me to leave and months were passing by, although I still enjoyed those trips to New

York City and the delicious food in the Hoboken restaurants.

There finally came a point in time when the backwards and forwards ended, and I personally took the contract of the designated new superintendent to the Executive County Superintendent of Essex (not Hudson, due to even more weeds) for approval and signature. Yes, that was the job yours truly once held for six years, and yes, again, the incumbent in the job and I had a positive collegial relationship. It was fun to see the new offices of the Essex Superintendent and greet a few former employees, but even better to leave with a signed approval of my successor's contract.

"Happy Days" – I could leave! It was now January of 2011. The Interim Assistant Superintendent was appointed Interim Superintendent, pending the arrival of the new superintendent, AND I was asked to remain on payroll part time to insure a smooth transition. I did, it was, and what was to be my final leadership role as a public-school educator came to an end 20 months after it began.

# Chapter 9

## Lawyers, Courts, and More Lawyers

"In medias res" wrote a very famous Roman poet, which translates into "in the middle of things." Or another way of phrasing it, "while I was doing that, this happened". As you have already observed, lawyers played a significant role in my career. On more than one occasion, they were instrumental in my employment; on another occasion, they were instrumental in my termination; on several occasions, they were instrumental in my working with them on several cases.

Men and women who opt to study THE LAW are most interesting creatures. They have learned to argue both sides of any issue, and argue either side successfully. They have no point of view, only the viewpoint which will win the case regardless of right or wrong. Having spent months and years dealing with these people, I developed some similar idiosyncratic views about life, liberty, and the pursuit of happiness. Furthermore, my six years as an employee of the State of New Jersey, wherein I was required to present and interpret the State's Laws and Codes as they pertained to education, placed me in a position where several of the State's prominent attorneys were eager to retain me as an "expert" for some of their trickier cases. As always, if the phone rings, I shall answer, and I shall respond.

So, for ten years, I flew the friendly [not always] skies of jurisprudence. The cases in which I was involved fell into several categories, but two primarily – school district disputes and institutional child abuse. Perhaps I best share why I became involved with lawyers as partners in the first place. Short answer – money! The hourly rate for your truly was quite adequate and all encompassing. Whatever time I spent working on the particular case was billable to the particular law firm and thus to the client. The time was primarily devoted to reading the narrative of the case, and then researching the law and code which were applicable to the situation and of course analyzing the actions of the principals (primary characters) in each case. This was particularly taxing in the child abuse cases, given the fact that there was always a victim.

Allow me then to share with you some of the cases in which I was involved after my Hoboken work, all of which I might add, we won, or at least did not lose.

The cases shall not be presented in any order of chronology or even by type of case. They will just be presented with reader option for conclusion or opinion. Let me begin with two institutional abuse situations. A school district must make every attempt to keep its pupils safe and free from assault and abuse. When an incident occurs where it is evident that a child's safety and security may have been placed in danger, a lawsuit is sure to ensue. In order to add legitimacy to the case from the education law perspective, a Peter Carter type is sought by the defending school district. In this case, a teacher was accused of inappropriate sexual behavior with one of his male students. After the criminal investigation, the teacher was charged. Simultaneously, the parents sued the teacher and the school district. I was hired by the attorney representing the school district so that the district would be held harmless in the matter. It was my job to bring to the court all the data pertaining to child abuse in the State of New Jersey, as well as all data created, produced, and promulgated by the school district. We had to convince a judge that the school district had done everything reasonable and rational to prevent staff from abusing students.

I prepared pages upon pages of proof that the district had taken all means possible to ensure that its employees were aware of all particulars with respect to child abuse, including memoranda, workshops, and proof of attendance at these events. Once shown in evidence, the district was off the hook with respect to liability for a suit. Once I completed my extensive work, my job was over, and I gratefully deposited my well-earned, lucrative check for services rendered.

So, you may wonder about the accused perpetrator and all. I do not know, nor should I. I am merely the technician here, not the social worker, nor the law enforcer, nor a family member. However, I trust there is an interest in the author's thoughts about institutional abuse. Needless to say, I abhor anything or anyone which hurts children, and expect that prosecution to the fullest extent of the law should follow. Also of concern is the therapy for the victim and the treatment of the person who has caused such harm to a minor. These are not simple issues, and there is always the possibility that abuse did not actually occur. Again, that part is for our friends in law enforcement "to get it right." My job is to produce data which absolves the school district, a legal entity, not any of the people involved. The reason I am successful at this is because I have no attachment to the human element whatsoever. For the record, the human elements in the case just described were all Caucasian, and the "expert" instrumental in the WIN was black.

Let me remain with this aspect of my post 2011 consultant's life. Another case in which I was instrumental in saving a school district from fiscal and reputational disaster involved a young girl and a school bus driver. You may need some support for this one, although I will attempt to keep the facts as tolerable as possible, as well as somewhat general to protect all parties involved. On a daily basis, a particular female 5th or 6<sup>th</sup> grade student was picked up at her home for transportation to school. It was alleged that the bus driver molested her on a regular basis for over a year. The driver, let's call him Sam, persuaded the parent of the young girl, let's call her Sally, to alter the pick-up time by fifteen minutes earlier. Sam then drove to a not yet inhabited parking lot, turned off the motor, and invited the child to sit on his lap and/or in the seat directly behind his. There was another male student on the bus who by all accounts was totally unaware of what may have been happening. It is alleged that Sam sexually molested the child in this parking lot and then resumed his route to pick up other children. I shall pass over the sociological circumstances surrounding the child's life, which clearly led to her victim-type posture. There was also a grandmother involved, although no male adult guardian figure in the picture. The mother, by the way, raised no question as to why Sam suggested a pick-up fifteen minutes earlier than necessary.

For months and months, Sally did not mention the alleged improper interaction between herself and Sam on the bus. There came a point in time that one day, while being driven to the movies by her friend's mother, Sally revealed what had been happening on the bus. The friend's mother, thank goodness, brought the story to the attention of Sally's mother, and also to the police. An investigation ensued, an arrest made, a lawsuit or two filed, and I was hired. It is essential to know that my expertise was based on my knowledge of school law (This was, of course, a criminal case.) as such pertains to the school district. My job was not to get into the weeds of the case itself, hence my success. It probably appears "cold" to the reader, but I only did what I was hired to do.

In this case, the bus driver, Sam, was an employee of a third party, the actual owner of the bus company, not the school district being sued, whom I represented. The school district had contracted its transportation needs to a "commission," quite a usual occurrence, who in turn had hired a bus company and its drivers. Thus, there was no nexus between the school district and Sam. However, I was able to demonstrate that the employees of this third party had been exposed to the rules and regulations with regard to institutional abuse. Yes, those workshops and other data had been shared with these third-party contractors, and I was able to demonstrate such. Once I had done the research and submitted my findings to the attorney representing the school district, my job was done, and I was summarily let go. Yes, I was paid (only partially unfortunately, but that's another story) for the thorough job I performed on behalf of the school district. I have no idea what happened to Sam or Sally or others in the case. All I knew as that I'd saved the school district from any wrongdoing.

One may query as to how a human being can be involved in a child abuse case, read all the "facts," but be aloof from the actual particulars. The law pertaining to institutional abuse deals primarily with how the institution prevents such abuse and what to do when such is discovered. I was able to show that the institution named in our aspect of the case checked all the boxes necessary. My job was done as far as the client was concerned; we won. I am not sure whether the school district knew what I looked like, although by then I was well known in New Jersey. Believe it or not, I never met the attorney who had retained me, although the internet did reveal a photograph of the white fellow.

We can reflect for a moment that race may not matter if you are good at what you do. Ah, there is that theme once again. Being good, actually being exceptionally good at what you do. In neither of the cases I just shared did it matter that the "expert" was black, white, or polka-dot. Nor am I certain whether the attorneys for whom I was working were aware of my race. Everyone was aware of my skills, which is really what counts. As you recall, I was told as a young child, whatever you do my boy, do it well. So, whether I put my emotional self into these cases was irrelevant; in fact, the less emotion, the greater the chance for the WIN. I admit putting forth the WIN as greater than the PERSON appears somewhat (or a whole lot) inhumane, but I was (and possibly shall be) hired to be victorious and save a school district and its insurance company from tens of thousands of dollars in claims for negligence and the like.

It is left to the other professionals to deal with the injured and the disabled, and I certainly hope that happens because that is very important. It is also important, though, that organizations are not successfully sued if said organization did nothing wrong. Back in the late 1950s/early 1960s, many of us watched "Have Gun, Will Travel" about a hired gun named Paladin who was contracted to represent whoever paid him, regardless of his point of view about the particular issue. As a matter of fact, we were never told his actual point of view. Well, just call me the 21st Century Paladin for some New Jersey school districts, and yes, I do have a card (I invite you to Google the western's theme song.).

# Chapter 10

## District v District v State Department of Education

Before I get into the details of my work in these cases, allow me to first explain (as simply as possible) how the State of New Jersey operates in terms of its 590 school districts. In New Jersey, the municipalities have decided upon several configurations with respect to the education of their children. The first and more common is the usual Kindergarten through Twelfth Grade (K-12) arrangement. Then we have the Ninth through Twelfth (9-12) set up, and then the Seventh through Twelfth (7-12). Don't hang up yet – there is the Kindergarten through Eighth (K-8) and the Kindergarten through Sixth (K-6). For good measure, let us add pre-Kindergarten to those districts which begin K-. So are you with me? Five different set ups to educate New Jersey's children! We shall not ask "why" because this is not "War and Peace;" this is "…Blackness Continues," a much shorter bit of writing. Now that I have given you the landscape, let us get into the nuts and bolts.

Most of the K-6, K-8 districts, which are called feeders (they feed into the 7-12 or 9-12 configurations), are quite content with their given status quo. Occasionally, (usually three-year intervals) the Board of Education of a feeder district becomes concerned about the education being offered at the receiving (7-12 or 9-12) district. When the district becomes extremely concerned and then disillusioned, it retains special counsel (a law firm) to seek a change in the relationship. Such a change can only be granted by the Commissioner of Education, after a recommendation by a person called an Administrative Law Judge. It is job of someone like me to successfully convince the judge, against opposing counsel, that the concern is valid and free from racial bias or animus. And yes, I am one of the few people experienced and smart enough to be what is called an "expert witness." The fact that I am black and smart is a value added, as you shall soon observe.

You recall from the prequel that I worked for six years as an education official for the State of New Jersey. In that capacity, I learned and administered the state's law and code as it pertained to education. The other thirty years as an educational leader did not hurt either. It became my job, in the several cases, to gather information both from paper and ground sources to convince the judge that my client (actually the client of the law firm which hired me) was correct in its concern and that a change in receiving district should be allowed. The "sell" was tricky, in that the new potential receiving district was populated by fewer black and brown kids than the current arrangement.

The first time I heard the term Feasibility Study was in 2013, a few years after my Hoboken gig. The term refers to the facts garnered about all the entities involved in the educational divorce and second marriage. There are several pieces to a study: the financial, the demographic, the instructional. Your author is the instructional expert. Gathering pages upon pages of data from school district, state and town websites, coupled with "on the street" work and visits to all the schools which encompass the district comprises my portion of the Feasibility Study. As the term intimates and implies, we are trying to determine whether a change would work and not cost either district pain or suffering in the pocketbook or in the population outlook. Any appearance that racial composition was at the base of the desire for change would produce a poor recommendation to the Commissioner from the judge. You can readily see how convenient it was to have an African American testify under oath that the desire for change was based only on the academic (teaching, learning) outcomes.

In my first case, this school district in the southern part of New Jersey sought to sever its ties from its existing send-receive relationship and to establish a new relationship with another school district. Actually all the cases I shall share will have a similar scenario. The current district to which our client had been sending its eighth graders for decades had become lax in many areas, resulting in a lessening of the academic rating of the district. The proposed new district had not only improved over the years, but it was excited about receiving its new students. I had unfortunately injured my knee, making my visitation to the high school very painful. Perhaps, fortunately, the original receiving high school did not permit me to visit. You may ask, "why?" The honest answer must be that it preferred that I not see its operation. I did make several requests and was refused each time by both the Superintendent and the Principal.

My first court appearance in a case of this nature was stellar. The judge recognized my competence and accuracy, and liked me. As I found out, the "like" part is very important in these cases, and the "like" grows from an abundance of preparation and poise. The court proceedings run about five days, and I personally spend about five hours on the stand in direct and indirect testimony. Opposing counsel's job is to cause me to contradict myself or confuse the facts. There is also an "expert" person representing the other side, by the way, whose point of view (and sometimes falsehoods) I must prove invalid (or wrong). From start to finish, a case usually takes 18-24 months from my first telephone call of engagement to the final decision by the Commissioner. A decision in the favor of the client, a change in the send-receive relationship is a WIN. The black guy is now one for one.

While I have your attention about school districts and their sometime disenchantment with their receiving counterpart, allow me to share with you some particulars of my next case, which began a year later than the prior situation. This time a K-8 school district in the northern part of the State of New Jersey wanted to part ways from its current partner as a matter of economics. Simply put, my client wanted a bigger bang for its buck, or a similar 9-12 education for its students for less money currently being charged by its receiving district. Another way of viewing the situation was a "land grab" by a neighboring district for a handful of eighth graders each June. To put it in even plainer terms, why buy a Wendy's burger when you can get a McDonald's burger for less money. A burger is a burger. Or is it? That's my job to find out. Perhaps there is a special sauce!

Since we are in northern New Jersey, Hudson County in particular, there are more political and other complications in the mix, which the "expert" must weed out and consider. To protect all parties involved, let us call the players District A (my K-8 client), District B (the current receiving district), and District C (the district desirous of new business). In order to establish a student baseline and the climate of the client, I spent time visiting the seventh and eighth grades of the elementary school in question. By general standards, this was a very small school in an interesting community. The political structure was predominately one ethnic group, but the student body was primarily Hispanic. The school itself was similar to a neighborhood parochial school, with very sheltered and protected young (for their age) kids. I should tell you at this point that the mayor of the community was married to the President of the School Board. Hey, it is northern New Jersey!

Once I had evaluated the nature of the elementary school, I visited the high school, which their older brothers and sisters attended and had attended for years and years. The match as far as climate and culture was unbelievable. The education offered was good, and the social interaction of the teenagers was very positive. The governance of the place was a different story, but then again, there is location, location, location. During this time in New Jersey, the Governor's salary cap for superintendents was in effect, and thus if a new contract involved a raise, and it always does, there are complications and definitely a non-approval by the State. Our "friends" in District B had pro [de] moted the incumbent superintendent to Assistant Superintendent, and promoted the Assistant Superintendent to Superintendent. There was no cap (ceiling) on the salary of an assistant superintendent. You get the picture — District B got around the cap situation in a very clever manner. You can imagine the meeting I had with the officials of District B. The District A meeting was no laughing matter either, given the unique civic positions (pun intended) of the key players. Clearly there were not too many secrets between the school leader and the town's leader.

District C was a free-wheeling type of place with quite mature teenagers, who had freedom of lunch at the eateries in their community and possibly some other freedoms too. The academic offerings were adequate and well administered; the co-curriculars were wide-ranged and even imaginative in parts. The school climate was to say the least, exciting. What a high school! But not, in the opinion of this consultant, for the children of District A. The children of District A were not ready for this type of secondary environment, and never would be. Thus, it now became my duty to persuade District B that it would be in their best interest to adjust their fiscal charges to District A. In addition to District B's circumvention of the Code, a count of their staff revealed discrepancies with the numbers it had reported to the Department of Education. For some reason or another, the Department had not noticed the difference – oversight or incompetence.

Another meeting was held with the [Assistant] Superintendent of District B, wherein I posed the reality that a second visit and examination of their personnel data would not bode well for all concerned. Tricky they were; stupid they were not. A pleasant "Mr. Carter, you will not have to return; we shall adjust our tuition" ended the proceedings and eliminated the need for our completion of the Feasibility Study. The send-receive relationship between District A and District B continued and shall more than likely continue for many years into the future. This was a win-win situation, so much so that the client wanted me to do some work with regard to their obtaining a building in town to better house the elementary school. It became somewhat apparent that the District was seeking some *pro bono* work on the part of this black man regarding the negotiations and procurement. I respectfully thanked the district for its confidence in me and declined the opportunity to work for nothing. It is my understanding that the district was eventually successful in buying and populating the more spacious building for educating its kindergarten through eighth graders, even adding a pre-kindergarten program.

For those keeping score, it is now two for two for education's Jackie Robinson!

# Chapter 11

## Recess from the Courts / Mentoring of a Woman

Do you remember a certain young lady whom I was [am] mentoring as she rose through the professional and academic ranks? By way of reminder, she (MVG) was the Cooperating Teacher whom I met when teaching at the college level. I believe I used the word "superstar" in that prior chapter, and here is why. You recall that I met this teacher in her fourth-grade classroom, dressed in the manner I believe a teacher should be, complete with high heels. Yes, a teacher should send a message to the students that they are worth "dressing up" for, regardless, of course, of the gender of the teacher. Look good for your kids, and they will perform well for you. It was a joy to be in her classroom as she taught her students in an atmosphere which indicated that they were very important, right down to a monthly display of birthdays for the month. I recall distinctly wishing one of the fourth-grade boys a "Happy Birthday;" he was thrilled. Unfortunately, the student teacher had never noticed the obvious display, and thus ignored a significant event in the life of this child. I could go on and on in the description of the teaching style of this outstanding educator, but the book is about me, not her. However, she absolutely deserves at least a chapter.

During one of my post observation conferences, I asked this young lady where did she see herself in ten years; her reply was as a Superintendent. I said "DONE." From her fourth-grade classroom, she went on to two separate principalships and wound up five years later as Superintendent of a very suburban school district in Essex County. You may also recall a certain black guy who was once the superintendent of this entire county. So, when it came time to making a recommendation and then finalizing a contract, the long since highly respected black guy prevailed. In fact, there was some drama when I proposed including a graduate school tuition clause in the contract. The drama was on the part of the candidate, not the board. She was afraid the board would reject my language for payment of her doctoral degree and dismiss her from the search. I told her that such would not happen. After all, she did inform me that she was interested in obtaining her doctorate before a certain age, hence the reason I included language toward that goal in the contract for her new job. The vote for the superintendency on January 6, 2010 was unanimous for this extremely attractive white woman, the wife of a white cop, the driver of a Hummer and then a Mercedes.

You may note that we have not checked off all the boxes for this female school administrator. We shall do so now. There is so much which can be written about this woman whom I mentored through many years of her career, but of serious significance is our conversation about family – hers and her husband's. June 13, 2011 and April 1, 2015 marked the culminations of all conversations on the topic of family.

By way of recap, we have one small suburban school district (wealthy and a pain), one husband (a daddy and a saint), and a pandemic (dangerous and a challenge). Oh, there is one more thing – the doctorate. Somewhere among training for and running in a New York Marathon, there was her admission into graduate school for the doctorate (December 2017). Yes, I was there, somewhere, for all of it. This elderly, retired African American educator remained on the MVG carousel for seventeen years, and perhaps more. The point of all this ink is to indicate that race does not matter when it comes to humanity and professionalism. It is not necessary to share an ethnicity in order to share a dream.

During the years of this woman's superintendency, I made some visits to the school district, and we held many conversations about the nuts and bolts and ups and downs. To say that she did an amazing job as a school leader is an understatement. To say that she hardly needed the black guy at all is a fact. She ran an outstanding school district, including a flawless virtual Sixth Grade Promotion Exercise (aka Graduation). There is no doubt in anyone's mind that this journey was a first for all the parties involved and, indeed, a story worthy of the tell. The relationship began as adjunct to teacher and ended as friend to friend. Yes, the blackness continues with indeed another major first, but it must be noted that we may have a white first here also – imagine that! It is about a word we have seen before in my narrative – Aretha's R E S P E C T. To move away briefly from the author himself to current social justice issues, racism does not necessarily run rampant through the streets of our nation. There are situations where humanity prevails despite the world around us, where some political leaders are proud to promote hate based on race and/or ethnicity. Let us not even go to the sexual harassment thing, also prevalent in these decades. The reality is that an older single black man and a younger married white woman can professionally coexist and excel as individuals and partners in education. The ultimate beneficiary is/are the elementary [young] and secondary [teenage] students – that is what the deal is about, after all, the kids.

# Chapter 12

## Back in Court – Almost – Then, Actually

After that second win, there were two situations which never reached court status. Let us set the year in 2016, when a school district was seeking to consolidate its buildings by one, given the fact that the district was educating children from two separate towns in a K-12 environment. To make a story which could have been longer short, let me state that the district's goal was just impossible. Any way I structured it, two plus two could not equal four. The challenge was to convince the townsfolk of the mathematical dilemma involved. Several of the taxpayers, however, were intent on putting a square peg into a round hole. Since I promised brevity, I shall avoid a narrative of the facts in this situation, other than to share with you, the reader, that there was no educational[ing] way our client's goal could be accomplished. Oddly enough, the district desired to hire me for an alternative "fix" to another situation. Their desire, unfortunately, was not supported with dollars, so NO DEAL for this southern New Jersey school district.

The next "almost" case takes us up north in the State of New Jersey. In this situation, a school district desired to open old wounds which had been litigated ten years in the past. This case absolutely involved race. Quite simply, the district, a K-8 arrangement which we represented, desired to no longer send their eighth graders to a high school which had become over the years predominantly minority. The case had been decided years in the past against the client based on racial discrimination grounds, but our client believed the racial conditions had changed. Of course, if the racial conditions had really changed (fewer black kids at the receiving high school), there would be no need to have retained us. An amusing side to the case occurred at our preliminary meeting with the client. The client's Board President, a highly respected funeral director, openly stated, "This isn't about race!" With a smile, I replied, "Of course not!"

I performed all the necessary work of research and high school visits, even though the current receiving school did not give me access. I even wrote a report. Now here's the rub: local politics on the part of the client intervened and our services as special counsel were suddenly no longer needed. There was also intervention of sorts by the district's regular attorney. So, this can be scored as a non-case due to outside intervention. It [stuff] happens! Never count those chickens while they are still eggs.

This next to final bit of jurisprudence I am about to share with you is shear artistry on the part of your black narrator and protagonist. The case involves three school districts, let us call them X, Y, an Z. School District X is an elementary K-8 school district desirous of changing its sending relationship from District Y to District Z.

Let us establish at the outset that the students in all three districts look alike – they are white. Here is the story. School District X wishes to provide its future 9-12 populations with a specialty type of secondary education not offered in District Y but indeed offered in District Z. Not only just offered, but offered well. It became my job to convince the Administrative Law Judge that the

Commissioner should grant a change in receivership to District Z. The data was clear and pristine that the children would benefit greatly from the type of instructional opportunities offered by District Z. My research into the situation was outstanding (The judge even said that.), wherein I convinced all the parties involved that District Y did not offer the types of career-oriented courses provided for the students at District Z.

The case opened with a surprising turn, wherein the opposing counsel initially attacked me personally in open court based on my age and my being too long removed from schools and school districts. Yes, there is a term for that – bigotry and discrimination! Once I pointed out to the court and to both counsels what he was trying to do at the very outset of the "trial," we proceeded relatively smoothly. I surmised that opposing counsel may have remembered me from my days as a County Superintendent when I ruled against a proposal presented by a school district in Essex County which he represented. This attorney also recalled that we were involved in the case about which I just wrote, which had a political crash landing, where he was Board Counsel. I suspect his ire against yours truly was more the Essex County stuff of the early 1990s wherein he did not prevail. It is now 2017 by the way. Lawyers hold grudges…white lawyers, it turns out, hold even greater grudges against black county superintendents.

We spent many days in court with "slight of hand" moves on the part of the opposition, including a rather weak report by the opposing expert witness. The key was my developed legal relationship with Her Honor over my time on the stand. The particulars of the case are relatively complex, but boring, so I shall not take you through all of that. Suffice to say that this old black expert beat the younger white attorney. Our client was granted the change to School District Z, and the students of District X are the better for it. Three for three, everybody!

# Chapter 13

## The Continuation Ends,
## Perhaps with a Bang AND a Whimper

Well, we are finally coming to the end of this, my second and final book, but I shall merely call your attention to the acknowledgements contained in the first book. Dr. Elizabeth A. Carter of AAPPEAL, and Fr. Joseph McShane of Fordham University remain as the both the cause and effect of my literary efforts and are thanked again. Also thanked and indeed appreciated are all the people whose initials have appeared in both books as well as the human beings whose initials are not here, but without whom the blackness would have never continued.

The fourth case I wish to bring to your attention is probably my last, as age takes its toll on my stamina and patience. We return to southern New Jersey and a small K-8 school district which retained us to assist it in ridding itself of a terrible albatross around its neck. For decades, our client's eighth graders had been assigned to attend a nearby school district which, to say the least, has been replete with educational and governance challenges. Quite frankly, this was an unfortunate situation, not only for our client, but also for the receiving district itself. Since the case is pending as I write, I am unable to share too many specific details, other than to state that my K-8 client is seeking to have its eighth graders attend a high school, actually a high school district, which far exceeds the current send-receive relationship. The opportunities for academic as well as social successes for the children are not even in debate here. Once again, the present receiving district did not permit my visitation, but the potential new high school did. Suffice to say that "on the ground" equaled and surpassed "on paper."

The fit for the boys and girls of the sending school district into the potential new environment is perfect, and we look forward to that reality. We can speak in such positive terms because we have learned that our adversary has "surrendered" without our having to go to court. Indeed, the current receiving district has publicly and officially announced that it does not wish to pursue any proceedings. I did hours upon hours of paper research and actual travel on this case over a period of well over a year. There came a point in time, however, when the opposition uttered "Uncle." I believe that the decision on the part of the current [January 2021] Superintendent and Counsel not to proceed was due in no small way to the reputation we had established in these cases over many years. There was no need to spend time and money on a case they were sure to lose. We are taking the matter directly to the Commissioner of Education, where we believe we shall prevail as victors. FOUR FOR FOUR for the still black consultant.

In February 2020, the world was told of a deadly pandemic named COVID-19. I travelled from Trinidad to the USA in 1946, and in 2020 face a life-taking disease to the tune of 550,000+ of my fellow-Americans as of St. Patrick's Day of 2021. It has been quite a journey, and it has been my pleasure to have shared it with you in a somewhat matter of fact type of way. To be black in America is different for each black person, albeit the same for many of us. The question I ask so often is WHY is the African American hurting as a group, and WHY certain African Americans are not. Those of us who pursued being the FIRST have survived the constant and ongoing racism that is the USA. We have even survived the virus which has statistically taken the lives of more black citizens than white.

There has been so much written about the plight of my brothers and sisters in America, and so many reasons put forth. However, the WHY is never fully pursued. Why are there not more "firsts" or even "seconds" for black folk here in the colonies. I am not skilled or educated enough to answer the question, but it is not asked enough in my opinion. I was raised in poverty by a single female parent. My children were raised by a single female parent. Thousands of black Americans have done quite well, but tens of thousands have not. WHY? There was nothing special, I assure you, about my low-income public housing dwelling in Brooklyn, New York which encompassed my childhood and adolescent years. I do admit that most of the boys and girls with whom I played and prayed as a child did not reach my outcomes. In fact, nationally, black kids did not reach these heights. But, did they even desire such outcomes? WHY NOT?

As I've spoken with African American students over the years, so many have told me that my path was not as difficult as theirs. Such was [is] not the case, but it is an easy excuse. Missing perhaps is that parent of whom I spoke and wrote in the first book. Someone must be there to strongly encourage his/her [grand]son, [grand]daughter to want something more than a gang membership or a baby. The blackness can certainly continue, if there was true blackness present in the first place. I have no idea how to do that on a wide scale, other than to encourage my brothers and sisters to avoid the dangerous slope of self-pity of the blackness and blame of the whiteness. It was James Brown who, so many years ago, tried to tell us to say it loud that "I'm Black and I'm Proud." And it is recently that we see and read, "Black Lives Matter." The true question is: "How do Black Lives Succeed"? How do more of us have "FIRSTS" and continue those 'firsts' into 'forevers'? Perhaps I should quote another recording artist from the past, "The answer my friend is blowing in the wind, the answer is blowing in the wind."

## Bonus Chapters: Unpublished Stories from Peter Carter's "Around Town" Column

Peter Carter's *Around Town* column in the *Cape Gazette* became a cherished part of the local paper, drawing readers in with stories that captured the warmth and spirit of the community. His words brought to life the familiar places, rich histories, and colorful characters that make small-town life so memorable.

The three articles featured here were written just before his passing, scheduled to appear in May and June 2023, with lively references to the upcoming summer season and its familiar rhythms. Although these columns never made it to print, we are honored to share them here as a tribute to Peter's enduring legacy and as a final chance for his readers to experience summer *Around Town* through his words.

# THE WEATHER
## by Peter E. Carter

One of the most common topics utilized to begin a conversation with a stranger is THE WEATHER. Over my many years on earth, I never quite understood why and how this was so common. I suspect it might be the neutrality and safety of the topic, except that if the words climate and change are added to the conversation, there may be some controversy. As we enter what is called Spring we feel even more at ease in engaging with a fellow human being about this topic.

"Oh isn't the weather pleasant today" we say to the person on line for a coffee container at Panera Bread. "What a nice day" (with a smile no less) is shared with the person we pass on the boardwalk. And the catchall, "Lovely weather we are having" can be heard throughout Milton and Lewes. Unless of course it is raining, putting such a damper on things.

During the winter months, there is a melancholy built into the weather conversation since it appears that colder weather and white flakey precipitation are not welcome visitors to the weather picture. There is that grumpiness in the tone when we strike up the weather conversation, a complaint about something we can do nothing about. So why do we (or actually you since I have no interest in conversing about atmospheric and meteorological conditions) see the need to open a conversation about the weather. It appears to me that there is some need to display some connection with the other person procuring his/her coffee, and what better avenue to peruse than the weather. The challenge for those of us less interested in this phenomenon is how to respond to the weather inquiry.

The polite and safe response is merely to agree with whatever point of view is expressed by the kind stranger. Yes, indeed, it is cold enough for me. I have found that feigning lack of interest in the outdoor activity translates to lack of interest in the person posing the weather observation. Now if one wished to pursue a possible new best friend direction, a response of comparison with a prior day may be in order. There is no telling what the nature of that reply may produce. My advice is to keep one's commentary short and simple.

However, as I am sure we are noticing (and have noticed) the topic of weather during spring (not necessarily summer) among us strollers or café regulars is one of more frivolity and needless to say warmth. Our entire beings have been filled with joy and hope as we enjoy the lovely weather. We come to the conversation with that unknown person with a more positive tone than we did in February. It must be the sunshine that puts a better spin on everything, thus allowing for a very positive weather conversation.

Dare I move forward in the seasons to the height of summer where that weather conversant will still approach a stranger, but often with a complaint about the number of degrees shown on a nearby outdoor thermometer or on the ever-present mobile telephone. "Hot enough for you, fella" may be the opening salve. To respond with any reference to "climate change" could change the entire tenure of what may have been a short, pleasant conversation. If the responding stranger is lucky there is a 50/50 chance that the next sixty seconds shall not be hostile, however care needs to be taken in the evaluation of the person starting off the "hot enough" conversation.

So an examination of our Cape weather conversations has brought us to the conclusion that such are wonderful ice breakers to be handled with care. The mystery is: what is the need to strike up a conversation about the weather in the first place? There is no need, but time has taught us that this is the safest, most pleasant, no degree needed, topic to share with a stranger. Whether we admit it readily or not, we do have an opinion on the topic, and usually wish we could change whatever the existing condition, especially if unfavorable in our evaluation, happens to be. The weather is also something we shall always have with us, and we know, unlike our spouse, friend, pet, or partner it is going to change.

# THE ANNIVERSARY
## by Peter E. Carter

As, fortunately or unfortunately, a so-called scholar of classical languages by virtue of my undergraduate major, I am quite familiar with the meaning and derivation of the title of this week's piece, As we would say, from the Latin for 'year' (annus) and 'turn' (versus), we are turning the year for some event or another. What is so strange about the current nuance of the word is that it brings about certain amount of fear and loathing, especially if it relates to an event involving two people who are involved with one another, and more so if they have exchanged vows and legal documents of some kind, and most important of all really love each other.

It is a requirement under some possible form of punishment that both parties involved remember the particular date, and recognize it in some way with jewelry, perfume, colorful foliage, or at least something from the Hallmark Corporation. Such seems rather simple until one or even both (rarely) parties forget. Let's use marriage as the focal point where for the first several years, the commemoration of that beautiful event is relatively easy to remember. As more years pass, and more events enter into the couple's lives, the danger of the wedding date skipping our mind increases. At the risk of being seen as picking on a particular gender, it appears as though we males are the more recalcitrant when it comes to the remembrance of THE DAY.

The question now arises as to why such a negative reaction occurs on the part of the person who did forget the date or the occasion. It appears that "doesn't he love me anymore" immediately enters into the mind and heart of the allegedly aggrieved party. I have no answer, other than to admit that I have been at the forgetting end of a twosome. In my case I recovered sometime during the day in question, but, yes, it was too late, and probably while changing a diaper. Let me put out a call to the ladies and the one or two gentlemen in the 'I forgot' category that mercy should first prevail in these set of circumstances. If not mercy, then at least understanding. NO TAKERS, oh well!

As we know there are many other occasions which involve an annual recognition, including the workplace, aka a job. The presidency of the United States comes to mind as well as the first day we opened the office. The good news here is that there are other employees capable of remembering the 365-day passage of time for us. Yes, I did skip a very important anniversary, also worthy of reaction either way if overlooked. I bet some readers have already reacted that I went to the job before mentioning in sacred terms THE BIRTHDAY. Yes, indeed, the anniversary of one's birth would precede in importance the annual commemoration of the opening of the office or a business. Again, though, there is usually more than one person to remind dad that junior's birthday is two days away, or the twins shall be six on Saturday. Or even, dare I say, Grandma's 90th birthday is tomorrow. I shall pass on birthday memory with regard to the couple with the anniversary memory challenge.

There are so many annual events in our lives, and those of our immediate family members including parent deaths, niece/nephew births, son/daughter engagements.

There are also national events, usually tragedies like 9/11 or 1/6 or Pearl Harbor. And then there are those little 'first' occurrences such as "mama," walking, self-feeding, toilet training, kindergarten. We number among other firsts, a car, a house, a pet, a fur coat. All these events and many more fall into an anniversary category, or at least could be considered to fall into such a category. I know I neglected personal engagements and first dates and kisses – please forgive me, I am a male.

So, my friends, as we approach June in the not too distant future, where annual events usually begin to be commemorated, let us check our calendars, our phones, with our parents and kids to be reminded of what we are expected to know – an anniversary!

## THE OCEAN, THE MIGHTY OCEAN
### by Peter E. Carter

Just about now we are thinking about trips to the beach if we have not done so already. That body of water out there, just east of the boardwalk is called the Atlantic Ocean, as we know. Beyond the point where the lifeguard sounds his whistle warning us that we have gone a bit too far is the rest of the world, the rest of earth. The Atlantic Ocean is the second largest ocean in the world. If we could swim due east the destination would be Lisbon, Spain or even Casablanca. As we traverse across the European landscape, we pass Barcelona and will eventually reach Rome and Naples in Italy. Of course, we rarely think of these European cities of wonder and culture when we are splashing in the waves and building sandcastles. However, beyond our view and our reach are some of the true treasures of the Atlantic. I do not intend to influence you to contact your travel agent as you read, but there is more to the Atlantic than we see.

Moving north there is Halifax, Nova Scotia and then Newfoundland and Labrador and Godthab in

Greenland. How often do we think of Greenland when at the beach! There is a whole world out there, and we are given the opportunity to share part of it each time we go to the beach. Sailing out there are the huge cruise ships with thousands of people aboard, having fun, especially as covid has subsided. We are sharing the Ocean with so many, with so much. This "Sea of Atlas" covers one-fifth of the Earth's surface separating the continents of Europe and Africa to the east from those of North and South America to the west. Swimming with us (certainly further out) therein is lobster, haddock, cod, mackerel, and many other seafood delicacies. Ah, the ocean is essential to our culinary pallets, and the restaurant industry, one of the biggies down here in Milton, Lewes, and Rehoboth. The Atlantic is also home to the green sea turtle and humpback whale. The sperm whale, bluefin tuna, giant shark, and crabs are also common in the deep ocean water.

Some more places of note we can think about as we enjoy those fries, were we to be able to swim that far south, would be Rio de Janeiro and Buenos Aires in South

America, and eventually Antarctica. In between dabs of suntan (or sun repellant) lotion one's mind could even wander to Ferdinand Magellan and Francis Drake, whose exploratory voyages in the Atlantic centuries ago opened new vistas to the people of Europe during that time, and ultimately to all of us in the nineteenth and twentieth centuries.

There is so much to ponder as we observe the Atlantic from our beaches here in Lewes, Rehoboth, and Dewey, even though it tends to be more pleasant to enjoy a Louie's pizza or Kohl's Frozen Custard, or the irresistible Dolle's caramel popcorn. Reading at Browseabout or eating at Robin Hood, walking through the antique store, is much more natural than thinking about what makes the beach the beach. But without the water, absent the ocean, there is no beach, of course. Thinking about our safe swim within the normal boundaries of our portion of the Atlantic is indeed sufficient for a fun day at the beach with family and friends.

There are many industries which look to the Atlantic Ocean or other bodies of water as a source of employment. We are familiar with television's "The Deadliest Catch" where we view exciting and unbelievable events at sea. The Viking Cruise commercial catches our eyes from time to time, and those hotel resort ads make us want to be elsewhere. And every so often, we do think about boat sales at Short's Marine. We tend not to include rain or other water weather events in our panorama of water wonders or water fun, but we do note that water is more around us than we realize, and that it takes us to places far beyond Rehoboth Beach.

# About the Author

A graduate of Fordham University with a Bachelor's degree in Classical Languages, and Hofstra University with Master's degree in Educational Administration, Peter E. Carter labored in the vineyards of both private and public school education from 1965 when he began as a Teacher of Latin and English at Nazareth Regional High School in Brooklyn, New York, until his retirement in 2004 as Superintendent of Schools in suburban Ringwood, New Jersey. Mr. Carter enjoyed to the fullest each one of his positions as he traveled across New York, Delaware, and New Jersey enriching the lives of the K-12 student population.

During his 36+ year career, Carter was the recipient of numerous awards for distinguished service in his chosen field as a school educational leader. Though retiring in 2004, he continued to be called upon to lend his expertise in education in Interim Superintendent roles, volunteering in the local elementary schools, and serving as an expert witness/consultant for several New Jersey law firms. Peter had also been busy serving in local leadership positions, which included two homeowner association boards and the board of the Delaware Botanic Gardens.

His passion for literature and writing continued to be enhanced by his published articles in his local Rehoboth Beach, Delaware newspaper, his 2020 autobiography- A BLACK FIRST, and his 2021 sequel - A BLACK FIRST: The Blackness Continues… where he shared the trials and tribulations of his 36-year working career and retirement life in education. Being the "first" in many situations, both books allow you to experience his journey of weathering the storms of racism and bigotry, and applaud his victories as he overcomes those obstacles. Done all for one purpose, to give children the best education possible.

Mr. Carter passed away on May 8, 2023. He is survived by his two children, two grandchildren, and many friends, students, staff, and formal and informal mentees.

# Other Books by Peter E. Carter

## A Black First (2020)
ISBN 978-1-7336455-3-9

Peter E. Carter shares his journey of weathering the storms of racism and bigotry to shine as a prominent educator in the State of New Jersey.

Learn about all his firsts....

## A Black First: The Blackness Continues... (2021)
ISBN 978-1-7336455-5-3

This book delves into Peter E. Carter's enduring advocacy for educational equity, chronicling his post-retirement roles and challenges as a Black leader confronting systemic biases, while inspiring readers with his perseverance and commitment to change.

## A Black First: Leading Through Educational Barriers and Biases (2024)
ISBN 978-1-960727-13-8

This edition retains the same powerful content as the original 2020 release of A Black First. The only additions are a new cover, subtitle and a heartfelt foreword by his daughter, Dr. Elizabeth A. Carter, reflecting on her father's legacy and the impact of his life's work.

**For this and other books published by AAPPEAL, LLC. Visit https://www.eac-aappeal.com**